The Elton Brand Story

A New Sports Legend Emerges in Ameri

By

Offie C. Wortham, Ph.D.

and

Fern Penna

Forward by
Governor George Pataki

Order this book online at www.trafford.com
or email orders@trafford.com

Most Trafford titles are also available at major online book retailers.

Printed in the United States of America.

ISBN: 978-1-4120-2832-5 (sc)
ISBN: 978-1-4669-1605-0 (e)

Library of Congress Control Number: 2012902471

Trafford rev. 02/10/2012

 www.trafford.com

North America & international
toll-free: 1 888 232 4444 (USA & Canada)
phone: 250 383 6864 ♦ fax: 812 355 4082

TABLE OF CONTENTS

FORWARD

We know what a great athlete Elton Brand is, but a lot of people don't understand what a great person he is. He was a serious student in high school, which was why he chose Duke for college. And now that he's been successful he's giving a lot back to the community through the Elton Brand Foundation to help other kids. Too often today some of the great athletes are not the role models they should be. I've always looked up to Elton Brand, and I think our young people can as well.

Governor George Pataki
February 12, 004

PREFACE
AND
ACKNOWLEDGEMENTS

No book can be written without the help, both direct and indirect, of many people. The first person I wish to thank is Elton Brand. Elton met with me and my wife Vivian prior to his moving from Peekskill to Chicago. During this meeting at his home in Dunbar Heights in Peekskill he gave me a magazine that featured him in a major article, and said that I should acquire some good insight about him from the piece. He authorized the book and we shook hands on our agreement to work together on his first paperback. I deeply appreciate the encouragement given to me by Elton to finish this manuscript.

I would also like to give special thanks to my friend Fern Penna for his encouragement, interest, and support.

It is a pleasant duty to enumerate here the debts I have accumulated in producing this book. My wife Vivian and daughter Janel did me the great kindness of reading the original edition manuscript in its entirety and submitting my efforts to conscientious scrutiny. The excellent hard editing of Betty Harkins, Joe Aronow, and Phyllis Newham uncovered and removed many of the writing errors unwittingly introduced by the author.

Personal encouragement, advice, and stimulation were received from the following during the many months of work on the original edition and I wish to express my debt to the following: Ken and Maryka Goldberg, Pete Seeger, and my cousins James Walker and Donald Christian.

My acknowledgements would be incomplete without mention of Govenor George Pataki and Vincent Vesce, both former mayors of Peekskill and close friends of Elton. I acknowledge my deceased mother, Mary Gladys, and my father, Lloyd Wortham for giving me life and space, and I thank my brother, Alonzo and my sister, Pauline for being positive role models in school, at work, and in their personal lives. The presence of my two older daughters, Leotte-Kieva and Joy, have been a constant inspiration in my life.

Willie Johnson was most generous with his offering of pictures of Elton in Peekskill prior to Duke. Thank you for your support and confidence. And thanks to Don Worthy for his picture of Elton, his sister, and his agent, David Falk. Also, my gratitude to John Shadle, the creator of the Original Elton Brand Fan website, for his pictures of Elton at Duke and for the picture of Elton as a member of the Chicago Bulls.

Without the constant encouragement and intellectual stimulation of my loving wife Vivian, this book would probably still be a "future project" instead of a completed and published work. It is only because of her insistence and general humility that she was not listed as the co-author.

Last, but not least, I'd like to acknowledge and thank my inner guide who keeps showing me the way toward truth and understanding.

INTRODUCTION

Vincent C. Vesce

Former City of Peekskill Councilman & Mayor

1982 - 1993

Year after year, the Peekskill High School Boy's Varsity Basketball teams were the one constant the 20,000 people of a small city in New York State could count on. In the 32 years since I entered PHS as a wide-eyed sophomore, the Red Devils had turned in only one losing season and one season with as many losses as there were wins. Every other season produced a team with a winning record and eight of those teams won the State Section 1 Championship.

Just as everyone in town would count on a winning season from the local high school basketball team, those who followed the teams most closely came to expect the season to end shortly after the Section Championship game. With all of its success, PHS seemed incapable of winning at the Regional level, having never won a game beyond Sectional play. Glens Falls, the site of the annual New York State Public High School Basketball Championships, seemed much further away than the three hour or so drive it actually was. As far as PHS basketball fans were concerned, Glens Falls was at least as far away as the place they made that "unreal" high school basketball movie about...Indiana. Then, in March of 1995, right before the community's collective eyes and ears, Indiana was moved to the banks of the Hudson River due to the efforts of three coaches and fifteen teenage boys including a sophomore who wore number 42.

Young Elton Brand had become the focal point of a very good high school basketball team and of our community's civic pride. The very same date (March 18, 1995) that the greatest basketball player of all time, Michael Jordan, announced his return

6

to the NBA after a 17-month hiatus from the sport, PHS was playing in it's first ever State Championship game. Elton Brand, only a sophomore, had become a leader of this group of young men. They willed their way to 22 wins, broke through at the Regional level and won a heart-stopping game through the State Tournament to get to Glens Falls.

Peekskill was winning the Class C Championship Game against Buffalo-Traditional High School by the slimmest of margins, one point, when Elton Brand made THE PLAY that brought an entire community together as one. With the clock winding down in regulation time, the player Elton Brand was guarding received a pass in very good scoring position, down low, just to the left of the basket. As he went up for a short, almost sure to go in jumper, Elton Brand made THE PLAY...a play that would come to typify his intelligence as a player and, in doing so, give Peekskill High School the opportunity to win the game. Elton had one singular thought in his mind...no way could he allow a field goal to be made...it did not matter how easy a shot his opponent had...he simply could not allow a score.

With two seconds to go, as the ball left his opponent's hand, Elton did the one thing he could and should have done...he fouled his man and in doing so, denied him the opportunity to win the game for his team with an easy bucket. Elton Brand immediately turned to his teammates and coaches, pointed to himself and mouthed the words "I had to foul". There was no doubt in his young mind and there was no doubt in the minds of the Peekskill faithful who were there in person or listening at home on the local radio station, WLNA. It was THE PLAY...the one that had to be made...the one that was made by the young sophomore wearing number 42.

Then it happened. The Peekskill fans who made the trip, about one thousand strong, stood as one, and created a roar that would have drowned out the sound of a Boeing 747 on takeoff. The same was going on in every car, tavern, living room, family room, bedroom and kitchen… wherever the game was being listened to on the radio back in Peekskill. Never had the Peekskill community been so unified in spirit and in purpose as they were at that very moment in time…all because young Elton Brand made THE PLAY that had to be made.

The first free throw had no chance. It was as though the noise level created by the Peekskill fans made it impossible for the ball to penetrate the air. THE PLAY, the fans and the community came together to block a foul shot for the first time in basketball history. The second free throw was made in spite of the avalanche of noise that the Peekskill community created in support of their kids. In reality, THE PLAY had set up the best the Peekskill team and fans could really hope for given the circumstances…a tie in regulation.

Of course, PHS won their first State Championship that evening, 94 to 85, by outscoring their opponents 15 to 6 in the overtime. Elton Brand scored 7 of his team's 15 points in the overtime period and ended the game with 31 points, 13 rebounds, 4 assists and 2 blocked shots. However, it was THE PLAY that I'll remember best and the young man that brought an entire community together by having the instincts, understanding and guts to make the right play at the right time. Little did anyone know, his best was still to come.

The Elton Brand Story

"Here at Duke, the team was the star."
Elton Brand

Elton Tyron Brand is a shining example of the success of the American Dream. From very humble beginnings in a public housing project, Elton emerged as the most sought after basketball player in the United States, if not the world.

Born on March 11, 1979 in Peekskill, NY, a quiet city of 20,000 thirty miles north of New York City on the beautiful Hudson River, Elton was raised by his mother, Mrs. Daisy Brand. As a young child he was sent to nearby Ossining, New York, twelve miles away, to live with his grandparents, Clarathea Brand and John Timms Sr.. He was only there for a few years while his mother was concentrating on her older son, Artie, who was Elton's stepbrother.

Mrs. Brand, a big woman at 6 feet, doesn't want the credit, and she shrugs and looks away when asked how she raised him so well. "To be a good parent, you feed him and nurture him," she said. "Give him a solid foundation. Love him. No secret to it. My role? I birthed him." She says her son was born a good person, with a kind soul, innate qualities for which she can't take credit.

"He was my baby," said John Timms Sr., Elton's step-grand-father. "He called me dad when he was small. I was the father he never had. My wife and I would fight over him. Sometimes he would sleep in my arms all night and wake up smiling at me." Clarathea Brand, his grandmother, died in 1991, and Timms, now 70 and a retired garment industry worker, still lives in the same brown-shingle home where they helped raise Elton.

Elton said he has no regrets over never knowing his birth father. He's not concerned about his father ever reappearing, even as his fame grows. "It doesn't matter either way," he said. "It's not a thing I'm looking for. I'm not worried about it because all I knew was my mom. If it was Father's Day or something at school, my mom would show up. I didn't realize my father was missing. I had my grandfather. My older brother was 9 years older. There was my high school coach. There were a lot of positive influences."

Upon reaching school age Elton moved back to Peekskill with his mother. He excelled from the start at Uriah Hill Elementary School and insisted he would be a basketball star. His first-grade teacher, Susan Bottesch, remembers suggesting that her largest student might prefer football. He said, "No, Mrs. Bottesch, just basketball." She said, "Kids always say they'll be stars, but his heart was in it in the first grade."

His mother can still remember when the curtain went up on the Christmas pageant of Uriah Hill Elementary School back in 1987. The memory still brings a smile to Daisy Brand's face. There was her son, a wide body then as now, complete with red suit and white beard.

"He was Santa. A black Santa," Mrs. Brand said. "He wore the whole get-up. They needed someone to play Santa, and he was willing to go along." His very good friend in that play was Emily Pataki -- Gov. George Pataki's daughter.

"They sat together, and they were in plays together," the governor said from his Albany office. "He was Santa Claus and she was Mrs. Claus in the first-grade school pageant. "I've known him since he was 4 years old."

Treyon Telford was one of Elton's closest friends, a 6-3 guard and former teammate on the Peekskill High squad that captured two state Class D titles. Telford vividly recalls the scrimmage before Elton's ninth grade, when Elton was the starting pivot man on the Junior Varsity team. On the opening tip, Elton leaped, flicked the ball over the court, got the ball back, executed a drop step and threw the ball down on two defenders.

"A ninth grader, drop-stepping and dunking over two guys? It was crazy," Telford said. "Crazy" Elton finished the scrimmage with 38 points.

In high school, Elton 's teachers wouldn't know he played ball until they read it in the papers. He didn't strut like a lot of schoolboy stars or skip class. He sat up front and worked, even in his final semester. "It's something I wouldn't have expected from anybody," said Tom Carroll, his math teacher. "I mean, think about it, he was already going to Duke. He had enough credits to graduate. But he wanted to learn, to improve his mind. I don't think I would have been in class."

When he wasn't studying, Elton spent his childhood on the playgrounds of Peekskill - the half-court with chain nets outside his apartment complex, then up at Uriah Hill and later the middle school. He was always bigger and better than the other kids. As a middle-schooler, he started playing with a tougher crowd, high school kids and older. The younger Elton was fouled at every turn, initiation-style. "It was like a rite of passage," his brother said.

Artie told Peekskill High coach Lou Panzanaro that his kid brother was a good prospect. But the coach wasn't overly impressed when he saw Elton play the summer before his freshman year.

"Elton was never a trash-talker, never sold or used drugs, none of that," said Brian "Buck" Cureton, who grew up two doors down from Elton in Dunbar Heights. "It's like he had this tunnel vision, always looking to move to the next level. Now Elton and his mom are going the distance together."

New York Governor Pataki
A longtime admirer of Elton Brand

According to an article by Brian Heyman of **The Journal News** in Westchester County, New York, the governor of New York, George Pataki, is a big fan of Elton Brand.

The governor used to be the mayor of Peekskill, where he also grew up, and he was also a basketball player at Peekskill High School. "Early on, I think everybody realized Elton was a special kid," Pataki said. "And it's not just as an athlete. He's a very, very quality young man in every aspect, including intellectually and the way he handles himself. One of the reasons I'm just so pleased with how well he's doing in basketball was because he has such enormous character. I just love watching him play."

The more Pataki spoke, the more he made it sound like this was the ultimate sports role model -- great player, great guy. "You look at Elton, and he's the type of person you want your kids looking up to," Pataki said. "There are a lot of athletes who are just that --just athletes. When you look at the broader perspective, you really don't want your kids to try to emulate them.

"But you look at Elton Brand, and whether it's excelling in school, being a person of high character, or his obvious tremendous talent on the basketball court, I think any parent would look and say, 'That's the type of man I'd love to see my kids grow to be.'"

When Peekskill traveled up to Glens Falls to play for two state titles in Elton's sophomore and junior years, the state's First Fan, the governor, was up there, too, rooting on the Red Devils.

And when they took that first title Elton and his teammates stopped by the governor's mansion in Garrison, on the way home. Pataki and Elton went one-on-one at the mansion's backyard basket. "I think at that point he realized that he wasn't ready for college yet," Pataki said jokingly. Actually, Elton blocked Pataki's shot. Eight years later, Pataki appears to be mulling whether to take a shot at the presidency. Meanwhile, Emily Pataki went off to college, at Yale, (where her father went to undergraduate and law school). She almost considered going to Duke.

Elton's success means a great deal to the people from Peekskill. "I think it just really gives us a sense of how proud we should be to have turned out such a wonderful young man," George Pataki said. "Peekskill has had a long, long run of outstanding basketball players to go through Peekskill High School, but never one with the skills and discipline of Elton."

Elton was a figure so renowned in this riverside city that the use of his last name was entirely optional. It's something we hear in Peekskill again and again, that Elton was the type of young man anyone would want as a son. Another thing one hears was that if Elton did not dominate under the basket, he would be a star on Wall Street or at IBM. And another: that it's easier to dunk on Elton than to find anyone who had a bad word with him, and finally, adults in Peekskill always expected the world of him. One could see it in his eyes, people say, that Elton would achieve and not slip up.

"He has this sincerity on and off the court, a characteristic you don't often see in a young man his age," said Vincent Vesce, a former Peekskill mayor, and now an official in the Pataki administration who watched him develop in the city's youth basketball programs. "He looked me in the eye when he talked to me, like an adult. His maturity was striking. It sounds corny, but it's almost like he's too good to be true."

Mrs. Brand, a retired social worker, insisted Elton become an expert at Tae Kwon Do, white robes and all -- "Everybody laughed at me,"

Tae Kwon Do was a popular Korean martial art whose name means "the way of hand and foot". It uses powerful hand strikes, blocks, and kicks as a means of self-discipline, spiritual growth, physical conditioning, and self-defense. Tae Kwon Do develops the mind, body, and spirit, and encourages a balance of knowledge, strength, and honesty.

The roots of Tae Kwon Do go back over 2000 years in Korea, but the modern name and form of the art was established in 1955 by General Hong Hi Choi. Jhoon Rhee became the first American Tae kwon do Master in 1960.

The mental and spiritual benefits of studying a martial art include greater self-discipline, improved concentration, better work and study habits, improved self-esteem, increased self-confidence and positive attitude, reduced stress, and increased levels of relaxation.

Physical benefits include improved reflexes and coordination; increased energy level, muscle tone, strength, and stamina; better balance and body awareness; weight control; and better general health. All of the above are critical factors in becoming a healthy person, or a star basketball player.

One way to begin to understand the extreme discipline of Elton Brand is to understand that the early training in this ancient Korean martial art gave him an excellent foundation for reaching any goals he might set for himself.

"I wanted to give him moral values, religious values, good

character values, because these values are self-supporting," his mother said. "But Elton was just grounded. It was more than me. It was the Lord. Elton just always had the incentive to do what he had to, to create his basketball skills, to go to school and produce. It was inside Elton to want to be someone."

Mrs. Brand told her son when he was growing up that if he didn't do his homework first; there would be no basketball. "Academics always came first. It had always been school first, then basketball," said Mrs. Brand.

It was a message that came through loud and clear. Today, as her son enjoys the status of being a national and international basketball star, it was his scholastic aptitude and discipline that enabled him to choose and succeed at an academically rich school like Duke University.

In addition to academics, Mrs. Brand also instilled in Elton the trait of never forgetting where he came from. When Elton was in the 9th grade, the Peekskill High School basketball team was eliminated from sectional competition. He and his mom went 40 miles north, to Glens Falls Civic Center anyway. The Brands went to the home of the state tournament, both to accept an award for Elton and see one of his boyhood friends, Shawn Tarkington play.

According to Mrs. Brand, they would have gone regardless of the award, because it was important for Elton to see his friend from elementary school compete in the state tournament. At the time, Shawn Tarkington was playing with the Section 1 champion Walter Panas Panthers, in Cortlandt Manor, who were competing for the Class B title.

In 1994, all of Peekskill was aglow because their favorite son, George Pataki, had just been elected Governor. Then, less than four months later, Elton would begin his ascension to stardom by leading Peekskill to their first-ever state championship.

Elton and George, both of whom have become two of Peekskill's icons, actually have a lot in common. Both are very intelligent, hard-working and humble people who are fiercely competitive in their respective arenas.

Coach Panzanaro

One would think that coaching Elton would be an extremely easy task and in many ways it was because of his work ethic, personality and his immense talent. But, Lou Panzanaro, Elton's coach at Peekskill High School, said, "It was recognition of that immense talent which made it difficult to be his coach. I placed a great deal of pressure on myself because I felt a responsibility to see that Elton reach the zenith of his developmental potential by the time he graduated from high school."

The coach wrote that practice sessions, drills, and off-season training regiments were designed to give Elton all the basketball instruction and knowledge he was capable of absorbing in each of the years that he was in high school. The coach developed a master plan for Elton, keeping in mind that he would have to progress through many stages. He didn't want to overwhelm him, but still wanted to keep him challenged.

In his freshman year, he wanted Elton only to understand the post game and establish two post moves. In his sophomore year, he expected him to increase his defensive intensity and presence. "We also increased the number of post moves with which he felt comfortable. In his junior year, we wanted him to become comfortable making moves from either side."

"People were already raving about Elton then," says Panzanaro. "But he was shy, pudgy. I didn't think he'd be ready for varsity. So I throw the ball up for the center jump, he tips to the wing, sprints to the basket, puts his hand up, gets the ball, drop-steps, spins, jams_with two hands, then nearly catches his own jam."

When the local paper started calling him a star, Panzanaro noticed his center growing lackadaisical "He was loafing, so we really put him through a grind. One day, Elton fell down. He was hyperventilating. He said he'd never play ball again." The coach was scared, so he called Mrs. Brand at home. "You ever get to know Daisy, you'd know Elton." She said: "Okay, you beat him down today. Make sure you love him tomorrow."

Eventually, two years later, Peekskill won the state championship. A lot of family and friends were in Glens Falls in March of 1995 when Peekskill finally won their first state title in the school's history. "They had a parade for the team. It was a big thing for Peekskill," said Mrs. Brand. Elton still passed up high school hallway adulation after leading his team to two state titles.

Artie, Elton's brother, remembers the time when there wasn't a soul around to see the top college player in the nation play. "I was just going out and playing with my brother. It was mainly a brotherly thing. He wasn't even a basketball player then. We just fooled around," said Artie, who was nine years older than Elton. "I didn't know he'd turn out to be as good as he was. But I knew he would be a good player because he was very athletic."

Artie always knew his brother would grow to be taller than him. "By the summer of '95 he had grown to be taller than me and finally beat me on the court," recalled Artie. "It was the summer before his junior year. It was a bad feeling (to be beaten by my younger brother), but it was like 'okay,' it's time to move on." Before Elton graced the headlines, his brother Artie enjoyed the spotlight, playing with Peekskill High School when the team won back-to-back league championships in 1988 and 1989.

Because he was an African American living in a racist

society, Elton could have developed an attitude that he was a victim of racism, discrimination, prejudice or even class antagonisms. But he did not do this. He was an excellent student in school, never got in trouble with the law, stayed away from the use of drugs, did not father any children out-of-wedlock, and developed himself into an outstanding athlete and basketball player. He was much more than just an oversize kid who had sidestepped trouble with a natural grace and ease.

Elton didn't hang out with the guys, not as a child, not even as a teen. He didn't hang out at Peekskill High School after class or after practice. He didn't hang with his buddies at the mall during the weekend, preferring to practice all day Saturday and after church on Sunday. And he didn't hang out at Dunbar Heights, the nice garden-type apartments where he was raised, and where his mother still lived until 1999. My sister, Pauline Hinton, a retired telephone company supervisor, had lived across the court from Elton for over 15 years.

When the outside lights flicked on at dusk, that was when Mrs. Brand expected her son inside, keeping out of trouble, not hooked to TV and girls, but hitting the books.

Of course he had his girlfriends and many hours of wild times that all boys go through, but Elton knew where to draw the line between destructive past-times and responsible behavior. "Elton's never been in any kind of trouble, nothing," said Henry Taylor, who grew up alongside Elton in Dunbar Heights. He always made his mother proud. He knew what he wanted to do and he stuck to his guns. He always had a clear goal and clear objectives." Some young men who were raised with Elton in Peekskill used their skin color and relative poverty to explain away their winding up in dead-end careers, in jail or on drugs.

"The difference between him and a lot of players his size was his strength and physical stamina," Elton's high school coach, Lou Panzanaro, said. "He's 6-foot-9 and 245 pounds. He's got a wide frame and was just very strong." Mr. Panzanaro wrote an entire article about Elton that appeared in the local newspaper, the Peekskill Herald. The following are some excerpts from this excellent tribute to Elton:

"I always questioned myself and wondered if we were doing the right things for him, because he was such a special talent. Elton Brand was arguably the best basketball player to ever play at Peekskill High School. I say arguably because Peekskill had a rich basketball tradition, which had produced so many great players and teams, However, no player that I'm aware of, had ever enjoyed the degree of success at the high school and then college level that Elton had achieved. Only Todd Scott scored more points in his high school career (2057).

"I first learned of Elton when I was coaching his older brother, Artie, in the late 1980's. Artie was also a hard worker who started at center on the basketball team. He used to tell me about his 10-year-old little brother, who was already six feet tall. A short time later, Pat "Guy" Donahue, a longtime fixture with the Peekskill Recreation Department, who also happened to be my recreation coach, came to me one day raving about the 46 points that Elton Brand had scored while leading Peekskill to a county championship over Mount Vernon in the Midget Division.

"The following summer I finally saw Elton first-hand, competing against kids several years older. The first thing that caught my attention was the large frame of this 13-year-old "man-child" and the exceptionally long arms. He certainly did hold his own that day. But entering his freshman year, I was not convinced that Elton was ready to play at the varsity level. I also had a senior, Rich Cotton, at the center position who had been on the varsity since his sophomore year, and who was a very talented player.

"Elton began his freshman year with the junior varsity team. Coach Art Blank then made a request that he would live to regret forever. He asked me to referee a JV scrimmage. Elton won the tap, sprinted to the block, received an entry pass, and jammed the basketball with two hands. He proceeded to score better than 30 points in the scrimmage and I turned to Coach Blank and said, "Elton just made the varsity."

The coach told him in a private talk that he was going to be up against some very strong competition in the future. This did not frighten Elton. "Coach," Elton said, "I'll do anything I can. I'll work hard enough to get to that level." And he did, staying after practice, soaking up everything his coaches said. Elton wound up receiving The Journal News player-of-the-year award as a junior and as a senior.

"The first thing that I would always think of was his intelligence and his poise and his grace and his concern for other people," Panzanaro said. "He was concerned for his teammates when he was getting a lot of attention. He didn't want to do interviews in front of them. He didn't want coaches to come into the gym to see him because he felt bad that his teammates weren't getting the same kind of attention."

Those years in Peekskill High were the beginning of an illustrious career that would culminate with Elton accepting a full scholarship to Duke University. In the interim, Elton became a starter two games into his freshman year. He led Peekskill to two public state championships and a federation title. He set a state tournament record by grabbing 23 rebounds in the Class B final against Rochester Franklin. Elton scored 35 points at Madison

Square Garden in a victory over Marist High School of New Jersey in a game billed as "The Elton and Felton Show." Felton was a highly touted St. John's recruit, but Elton dominated the game.

Elton also had a career-high 43 points against Salesian High School of New Rochelle in a game played at Iona College. Elton scored 2027 points in his career, pulled down more than 1500 rebounds and blocked over 300 shots. Because of Elton's high profile from attending such camps as Five Star and Nike, and playing AAU ball in the summer with Riverside Church, he was invited to tournaments in Florida and Kentucky, where he competed against nationally ranked teams.

Soon the big-time colleges were calling, and Elton had to make a decision about his future. An A student with SAT's of over 1100, he was drawn by Duke's academics. Elton had long been a Blue Devil fan, spurred on by his older brother's rooting interest. "It was kind of planted in my head early on," he said. "It was just embedded there."

Team, is a word that seemed to come up frequently when Elton spoke. Panzanaro had seen what Elton could do for a team over the last four years, and he had no qualms about recommending his player for any team in the nation.

"There's something special about the way he always carried himself on the court and in the classroom," the coach said. "He's just a very mature young man who happens to be a great basketball player." The coach has offered much insight into who Elton really is. He wrote that the goal for Elton in his senior year was to be ferocious on defense and to begin to be able to shoot effectively from the three-point line. "We also wanted him to handle the ball well enough to take people off the dribble."

The coach had few lingering doubts about Elton, but any

that may have been there dissolved in a game where Elton had a tooth dislodged. He simply stuck it back in place and played on. The tooth was smashed back parallel to the roof of his mouth. "Grossest thing I ever saw." said coach Lou Panzanaro. Elton recovered from that in about 30 seconds. Whatever pain he had, he just ignored it, Panzanaro said. "That's where Brand really grew up. He went on and had 21 points and 15 rebounds. I knew from that moment he was going to be a pretty special kid."

Panzanaro talked about how much kids looked up to Elton when he was here, about how much teachers loved him, about his 90s average and devout church-going ways. He had the full package: talent, intelligence and humility.

In the fall of 1996 he became the last of the Duke Blue Devils' incoming freshman class to officially sign his letter of intent, joining Battier, Burgess and 6-foot-2 point guard Avery to pick Duke as their choice for college.

Panzanaro agreed that Elton's prowess on the boards was due to more than brute strength. "He's a good rebounder," the coach said, "because he's got a nose for the ball and he's studied where shots are taken from and where he needs to be to rebound them." Despite his physical bulk and seven-foot, four-inch wingspan of his arms, Elton didn't believe he was guaranteed his share of rebounds. "You've got to work to go get the ball," he said. "You can't be nonchalant and let someone else get it. You've got to go after it yourself."

"I believe in developmental maturity," the coach said. "When he was 14 he had his first varsity experience, and he was six-foot-five or six but he still had to develop his footwork. He's been learning every year. He's developed mentally and came to understand what he could do on the basketball court." Over the summer of 1994 a whole lot took place. He was growing into his body, and he started to understand more of what it took to be effective offensively.

The overall goal of Panzanaro was for Elton to be as well prepared as possible to step in and compete immediately at the Division I level. When people ask what was it like to coach Elton, Panzanaro says that it had been rewarding, and he was proud of what Elton has accomplished. He felt very fortunate to have had the opportunity to have coached such a tremendous person and to have been able to share a small part of that experience with Elton and his family as well as contribute a little to his overall development.

Panzanaro wrote that the recruiting process was another experience, one that he would never forget. By his sophomore year, Elton already created a lot of interest. Hundreds of schools were inquiring about him. The phone rang constantly because NCAA regulations prevented them from contacting him directly until September of his junior year. Panzanaro asked Elton for some guidance to eliminate some of the schools that were constantly calling. He needed to know if he had any serious interest in them. The only guidance Elton gave at that time was, "Coach, California's too far and New York was too close," Needless to say the phone continued to ring from all over the country.

However, they soon established a plan of attack and slowly narrowed down the schools. By September of his senior year, there were eight finalists. From that point, they set up home visits and campus visits. Even though he decided upon Duke in time for the November signing period, Elton decided to hold off on the formal announcement until the spring. Panzanaro doesn't think anyone would doubt that Elton made the right choice of schools.

As Panzanaro looks back, he says, "It was extremely time

consuming, but also enlightening and fun." He got to meet and talk with coaches that until then he had only seen on television. He remembered Elton listening so intently as each coach spoke, and the intensity of the coaches, especially Coach Krzyzewski of Duke, as they sang the praises of their respective schools and told Elton why their school was best for him. His mother also sat through the whole process, and they both asked the coaches some tough questions. Elton was fortunate to have the guidance of his mother and Coach Panzanaro, because he did have to make some difficult decisions and weigh a variety of factors.

On November 7, 1996 Elton Brand officially announced that he would attend Duke University. In June of 1997 Elton Brand Graduated from Peekskill High School with a nearly A average. In high school, Elton had accomplished the following:

- Earned four letters in basketball
- Lettered one year in football as a tight end
- First-team Parade All-America in 1997
- Tabbed second-team USA-Today All-America as a senior
- A finalist for Naismith National Player of the Year
- A finalist for Gatorade National Player of the Year
- A finalist for the Morgan Wootten Award in 1997, an honor which was given annually to a deserving player who was a strong student and a community leader
- MVP of the Capital Region
- Participated in the McDonald's All-America game, collecting 16 points and nine rebounds in 17 minutes
- Selected to the USA Junior National Select Team that played in the Nike Hoops Summit
- Named the Gatorade State Player of the Year as a senior

- Four-time all-league, three-time all-county, and two-time all-state
- Three-time league MVP
- Two-time county MVP
- State MVP his senior year
- Team captain his junior and senior campaigns
- Recorded a four-year high school record of 80-18
- Averaged 25.9 points, 16.2 rebounds, and 6.0 blocks his senior year in leading the team to a 17-5 record and the league championship
- Averaged 26.1 points, 16.8 rebounds, and 7.2 blocked shots as a junior, leading the team to a 23-3 record and the league, county, and state titles
- Averaged 24.0 points, 12.0 rebounds, and 3.0 blocks his sophomore season as the team went 23-4 and won the league, county, and state
- Scored a career-high 47 points against Salesian High School
- Set Peekskill and state record for most rebounds in a game, accomplishing the feat in the state championship contest as a junior
- Scored over 2,000 points, grabbed over 1,200 rebounds, and blocked over 450 shots during his career.

Duke...Fall 1997

Opposing teams thought they might be able to breathe a small sigh of relief: Elton Brand, the inexperienced freshman, might not even be in Duke's starting lineup in the fall of 1997. The Blue Devils, many hoped, would probably be able to go 12 deep, with a glut of talented players in the front court. Duke would probably go with rising senior Roshown McLeod, who had started at power forward much of the past season.

"Roshown's a good shooter and slasher...I'm going to get to go against him in practice," Elton said in the summer of 1997. "He'll be a senior and gives a lot of leadership to the team. He's more of a slasher and a passer but I'm just going to have to practice hard. I can handle the ball. If I don't, it's not that I can't, but it's easier, and if playing inside was what the team needs me to do, I'll do it."

Elton knew when he committed to Duke that he'd face stiff competition for playing time. While other players might have chosen a school where they could star right away, he looked at the Blue Devils' talent as a plus. "Elton was well aware of it," Panzanaro said. "We talked about it in depth and his exact words were, 'Coach... I want to compete against the best players in college. What's wrong if they're all at Duke?' "

Elton would also have to compete with his classmates at Duke for time on the court. At the very least, the recruiting class of William Avery, Shane Battier, Burgess and Elton were considered by most college basketball analysts to be the best in the country for the next year-some went as far as to call it the best of all time.

"I don't think there's any pressure," Elton said. "We want to get in and be part of the team. I've talked to the other guys and we just want to fit in. We don't want to be our own little entity but a part of Duke basketball. There's not going to be any jealousy or hatred if you're part of the team. And they already have a lot of good players, so it's not going to be just us, but the whole team."

Elton had to play with and against his fellow signees in several previous high school all-star games. He had even roomed with Battier at the McDonald's All-American game, and with Avery at the Capital Classic. Elton said he had a good time hanging out with his future teammates off the court, but he still managed to outshine them on the court. He put up 16 points and nine rebounds at the McDonald's game and won Most Valuable Player honors at the Capital Classic for his 22 points and 11 boards.

But it hasn't always been that way. While Avery, Battier and Burgess have been considered top prospects for years, Elton failed to gain the same elite status until the summer of 1996. He attributes this to Peekskill not being a national high school power known for producing college standouts, pointing out that Battier, for example, attended Chris Webber's alma mater.

"The recruiters just had never seen me," Elton said. "I needed the exposure and that's what happened at the big camps. It was my first time at the Nike camp and I played in the national AAU tournament too. If the scouts couldn't see me they couldn't rate me." Panzanaro added that Elton had shown tremendous growth as a person and player over the last few years.

"The American Dream was alive and well and being nurtured by every dribble, jump shot, and rebound that basketball whiz Elton Brand performs. That dream had a special reality for many children and young adults who, like Elton, were growing up in Peekskill." So wrote Sally Bentley about Elton Brand.

She said that he may be on the cover of Sports Illustrated, and in the weekend sports highlights now, but not too many years ago he was sitting in Mrs. Bottesch's class at Uriah Hill Elementary

School or working on a Shakespeare paper for Peekskill High School English teacher, Kevin Dwyer. "Yes, there are a few first graders who don't know who Elton Brand was, but they won't get to second grade without hearing a classmate or teacher talk about what Elton did in a game over the weekend. Kids in Peekskill step a bit higher, hold their chins a bit prouder, because they have a chance to walk in his (rather enormous) footsteps."

When Sally Bentley showed visiting children in the Peekskill Field Library Children's Department that they could find Elton at several sites on the Internet, they were interested, but not surprised. "We know, he's famous," Danny Rivera instructed her one day. "And he's from Peekskill!" Danny attended third grade at Elton's alma mater, Uriah Hill. He couldn't see a Duke basketball game on television without hearing the announcer relate the achievements of "Elton Brand from Peekskill, New York." Kids know that Elton had seized the dream and they were happy to cheer him on. "And these kids felt entitled to dream their own versions of their successful futures."

Ten-year-old Michael Smythe and nine year old Javier Herrera had only seen Elton play ball on television, but they know that he's great at "dunkin' the ball and getting lots of rebounds." Both were Woodside students in Peekskill, in Mrs. Ruller's fourth grade class. Michael figured that Elton got to go to college because "he's so good at basketball and he gets lots of money." Javier emphatically corrected him, "Elton's smart. He had to be good at everything to go to college, and he doesn't get paid." Michael and Javier already knew that they wanted to go to college, but that it was going to cost a lot.

Fifth grader Molly Squires had been playing basketball with the Peekskill Recreation Department program since she was in first grade. She learned about Elton from her grandmother,

Barbara DiMartini, who loves sports and her dad, George, who's taken her to see Elton play. "I love to shoot baskets the most, it's my favorite thing," Molly said. "Elton's so good at shooting. I know that he's practiced and practiced," she told Sally Bentley. "So what do you think about him?" Sally asked. "Oh, I think that he's really, really good. He's so talented. I like seeing him doing so well. He's really inspiring."

With all of Duke's high-profile recruits and returning vets, Panzanaro wasn't sure Brand would get much playing time at Duke. "Maybe you'd prefer we just stop recruiting him," a somewhat angered Coach K suggested to Coach P. But feelings were soon soothed. And Elton reasserted his own confidence. "Coach K told me he didn't recruit me to sit on the bench," At first, I was surprised. Then I got cocky. People kept saying I should worry about Battier and Burgess and those guys. But I said, 'Wait a minute. Maybe they should worry about me."

In early scrimmages at Duke in 1997, there was plenty to worry about. Players know who's good, who's great, who should get the ball, who's emerging. Elton separated himself from the others right away. It was probably hardest for Chris Burgess. But it's no disgrace to play sideman to Elton Brand. One could build around his personality, not just his talent. He pulled guys' strings, pushed their buttons, found common ground.

"We developed so much respect for Elton," says Burgess. "He remained the same even after all the attention. He looked in the mirror and it was still him." Battier, who was a roommate of Elton at Duke, agrees. "We all knew there'd be times when different guys would take the spotlight," Battier says, "This was a brotherhood. There's no envy. We're all supportive of one another."

Battier said, "I think Elton's loosened me up somewhat. I was set in my ways, had to sleep certain hours. Now he has me up all night playing video games."

Fans at Duke are known as the "Cameron Crazies." They take over the Cameron Indoor Stadium with antics that amuse and delight basketball fans throughout the country. It's fascinating to watch the coordinated efforts of over 2,000 fans. When the announcer introduced players on the visiting team, the fans would all pull out newspapers and start reading, showing no attention to the opposing team.

Elton, Willie Johnson, and the Governor

They hoisted "Tickle me, Elton" and "Branded for Life" signs and screamed "I've Been Branded!" when Elton played. They called him the "E Train," Runaway Train and the Space Heater. But the hype of fans and media didn't phase the court star.

Mrs. Brand said that she's been especially proud of the opportunity to see her son play in such places as Madison Square Garden and Duke's beautiful Cameron Indoor Stadium. "I sat with all the other mothers at the game and we all felt a lot of gratification," said the proud mom. His mother spent much of her time in 1997 and 1998 in Durham, N.C., keeping an eye on her son, although she kept her apartment in Peekskill.

Following a defeat at Michigan in December, Krzyzewski reviewed Duke tapes during Christmas break and discovered the obvious: Elton was so good, so overpowering, so dominant--even when he wasn't the focus of the Blue Devil attack--that the Blue Devils had to change their entire offense. "We told the kids that," says Coach K, "and everybody agreed. "We were developing new drills - get the ball to *him*. Changing substitution patterns--to revolve around the guy was not just a bust-'em-up, low-post player. He was going all over the court, if the team had a race up court and back, the 270-pounder would win. Elton didn't even know how good he was: I did." Elton came so far so fast that just 11 games into his freshman season he was already the focal point, of the Blue Devils' offense at Duke.

Despite playing just over half a college season, he was already being touted as one of the best basketball players in the country, the near-unanimous ACC Player of the Year and possibly the first men's basketball player at Duke to leave early for the pros.

"It's all definitely surprising because I'd definitely say I'm unproven right now," Elton said. "I haven't played half of an ACC season and I'm up for ACC Player of the Year. It's an overwhelming jump that the media has made, but I'm looking forward to the challenge of just playing better and challenging myself."

"In 30 years, this kid was the best Duke basketball interview I've ever had," says Frank Dascenzo of the <u>Durham Herald-Sun.</u> "He's ridiculously mature: And Duke coach Mike Krzyzewski mysteriously avows: "Elton was run by a highly developed, internal intellectual system."

"Elton was genuinely interested in the world and how it works,' said Duke associate head coach Quirt Snyder. "He may not listen to my Miles Davis CD, but he wants to know about it and why I like it."

During an early-season lull in Elton's performance that Krzyzewski attributed to a bit of complacency that set in after Elton's gold-medal contributions in the U.S. triumph in the Goodwill Games Elton found himself pulled from the starting lineup for two games. Elton, a sophomoric center, received a wake-up call when he was informed that his lack of conditioning was hindering his game. He responded with 10 double doubles in the next 15 games.

After that, Elton was possessed, and the coach delighted. "He's been consistently excellent, and he's going to get better," Krzyzewski said,

However, on December 27, 1997 Elton Brand almost ended his career as a basketball player. "I thought it was a minor injury. It was upsetting. It was a helpless feeling watching on the sideline," Elton said, recalling that night. He had broken the fifth metatarsal bone in his left foot in practice two days after Christmas--the one that enables humans to do things like walk. "It was so sad," said Krzyzewski, "because he was on the verge not only of becoming a special player, but finding out himself that he was special. His was a very, very serious injury," Krzyzewski said then. "It just takes longer than a smaller man. The weight load that you have on that part of the foot was something you have to be careful with. In my mind, he was not coming back."

Things were different in Elton 's mind however, as he worked diligently with the school's medical staff to accomplish a miracle. "I had a feeling in the back of my mind that I'd be back," Elton said.

Elton had already made a difference for Duke and doctors should get credited with an assist. Health Team Medical Expert Dr. Allen Mask explains how ingenuity and new medical technology brought Duke's freshman star center back from a broken foot in record time.

Early in February, the cast came off Elton's foot, allowing him to shed crutches and walk with his left foot in a running shoe. It fueled speculation that Brand might return for the post season, but Duke seemed to rule it out. But Elton was determined to return to the game. After shedding the cast, he started running, and then practicing. The foot held up.

Orthopedic surgeon Dr. James Nunley said the break was a "Jones fracture." "The problem with the Jones fracture was the blood supply to the bone was in jeopardy because of the break." A cast could have been used, but instead Dr. Nunley tried a revolutionary two-prong approach. First he operated and put a screw in Elton's foot.

"We had to put one of the biggest and strongest screws we had to get the bones to get squeezed together. When it gets put into the bone it would squeeze the bone together and help re-establish the blood flow."

And then, the treatment got really innovative. To help the bone mend even faster and get Elton back in the game sooner, doctors used two new medical devices. The first was an ultrasonic bone stimulator. The doctors put it directly on the broken bone. It puts out a sound wave that Elton couldn't hear, but this wave actually would induce genes and mechanical changes in the bone that would cause the bones to heal. Elton used the device 20 minutes every day. He also slept with a device on his foot every night. This was the EDI pulse electromagnetic force bone stimulator. This created an electric field so that one end was positive and the other end was negative and it created a current in the bone and caused new bone to grow. An x-ray taken afterward showed that Elton's foot had healed perfectly, and was even stronger than before he broke it. Doctor Nunley felt the team approach to Elton's treatment was the key to his success. "What we've learned was like Coach K says, the basketball team wins the game, and here it was the medical team that won the game with Elton Brand." Now the only question was whether it would help Duke win a national championship.

He returned to the court on February 22, in a substitute's role while he built his stamina. When he entered six minutes into the game against the University of California at Los Angeles, he was just a freshman - but he received a standing ovation from the home crowd in Durham, NC "It's a feeling you don't have very often," Elton said of the cheers.

Watching Elton muscle his way to the basket, one would never know he had broken his foot December 28th. As Elton returned that night against UCLA, it was as if Elvis had returned to the building. Elton admits he wasn't as fluid on the court then as he was during the first month of the season. "Of course being out those two months, just having to sit around, it really humbled me," Elton said. "And the hunger, just wanting to play and not being able to was also very trying."

Duke triumphed 120-84 in that game, and Elton played 16 minutes, scored 14 points on 5 for 7 shooting, and grabbed 7 rebounds. But the most important thing was that he had no limp. It was still amazing how he recovered from a broken foot in two months when the normal rehabilitation time was four months. "I was just happy to be a part of the team again. After being on the sideline cheering for the team, it was good to be back. I didn't know what my role would be; I knew it wouldn't be the same role as when I left. But I was just happy to be back."

Even though Elton was back on the court, his treatment continued until the end of the season. He used the bone stimulators every day. He also wore a special device in his shoe for extra support. The injury cost Elton 15 games, the heart of his learning period.

As for the screw, it would remain in Elton's foot forever. To watch Elton Brand today, one would never know he was ever injured.

On Feb. 28, just as his team was about to be wiped out a second time by the evil empire down the highway at North Carolina, Duke's freshman center put his ultimate Brand on the Season. (Three weeks earlier, Elton had to watch sullenly in street clothes as the Tar Heels administered a 97-73 butt-whup in Chapel Hill.) The visiting Heels were rolling again, ahead by 17 points with less than 12 minutes left. Over the rivals' long and storied competition, seldom had the visiting team dominated the home team like this. And, with a share of the ACC title at stake in this regular season finale, the Cameron Crazies had never seemed so embarrassed, not to mention silent.

That made it all the more electrifying when Elton, only six days after returning to the lineup, simply took over the game and, in the process, inaugurated a whole new era for Duke.

Forcibly posting on the low block and rimming his enormous body through the key, the rookie took the ball up, over and through the Tar Heel defense, scoffing five times in six possessions, and forcing his veteran Carolina counterpart, Makhtar Ndiaye, to foul out. Elton finished with 16 points and, even more important, helped hold Antawn Samison to a single tip-in over the final 11 minutes. He scrambled to foul seven-footer Brendan Haywood on a point-blank chip at the buzzer that would have meant overtime. Duke rallied and won, 77-75. Cameron erupted.

Elton never slowed up from then on, and was named Associated Press honorable mention All-American as a freshman, despite missing 15 games during the season.

During that season:

- Elton played in 21 games with 18 starts and led the team in rebounding at 7.3 rpg
- He was leading the team in scoring at 16.0 ppg prior to his injury
- He finished the season third at 13.4 ppg, was second on the team with 27 blocks, getting at least two in 10 games
- Was named to the All-Tournament Team at the Maui Invitational
- Scored in double figures 15 times, with season-highs of 23 points against Chaminade and North Carolina-Greensboro

- Posted double-doubles against Michigan, Mercer and Syracuse
- Grabbed season-high 14 rebounds vs. Syracuse in NCAA South Regional
- Scored in double figures in each of his first seven collegiate games
- One of only six freshmen under coach Mike Krzyzewski to average in double figures in scoring, with Johnny Dawkins, Mark Alarie, Grant Hill and fellow 1999 NBA draft hopefuls Trajan Langdon and Corey Maggette
- Hit 100-of-169 field goal attempts (59.2 percent)
- Led the team in field goals made, free throws made, and free throws attempted before suffering the injury
- Averaged 23.5 minutes per game to rank fifth on the squad
- Averaged 1.5 steals per game
- Led the team in scoring seven times and rebounding 12 times
- Scored in double figures in 15 games with four games of 20 or more points
- Blocked at least one shot in 14 games with more than one in 10 contests
- Recorded back-to-back double-doubles against Michigan (12/13) and Mercer (12/21), then added a double-double against Syracuse

Elton giving thanks back to the community

Mayor John Testa proclaiming Elton Brand Day

Former mayor Vincent Vesce and Elton

Elton, his sister, mother, and agent, David Falk

Elton and his friend Governor Pataki

Elton and buddy Al Hammonds

Elton, Don Bennett and Wesley Bullock

Elton with friends looking at an Elton banner

Elton in a final championship game in high school

Elton at the Final Four

Elton and team after a victory

Elton trying to look mean

Want to come and try and get it?

Should I spin, or just drop it in?

Do you really want to mess with me?

This was really hard work!

Not tonight baby!

Sorry about that

You're in my way

I wonder what we're having for dinner?

You don't mind if I block that, do you?

I think I'll like Chicago

The 1998 Goodwill Games

In the summer of 1998 Elton led **Team USA** to the gold medal at the Goodwill Games. Elton's sudden recognition by many people seemed to take place during those Games, when he averaged 17 points and 7.6 rebounds in leading the United States to the gold medal. That's when much of the national media became aware of him. He already had a strong reputation by then, but suddenly the freshman who displayed as much potential as any Duke player, was about to be a sophomore with as much promise as any player in the country.

"The Goodwill Games were tremendous for Elton Brand," said his former coach at Peekskill High, Lou Panzanaro. "Everybody had said that he was a great player, but he was not a great player last year. He was going to be a great player when he got hurt, and then at the end of the year he wasn't a great player, but a good player that wasn't in top condition. The Goodwill Games gave him an opportunity to know he was a great player. It's not hype or anything anymore. Doing was the key, and that's the biggest thing that happened to Elton that summer."

Elton's fantastic playing in the Goodwill Games demonstrated just how good he could be. Rumbling against taller, more polished foreign professionals, he led the team in minutes, rebounds and shooting percent-age and was second in scoring as the U.S. team won. "Even when I played pretty well at Duke coming back from the injury, I never felt comfortable or confident, said Elton. "I had lost touch. I didn't know where I fit in. The team had a separate identity without me, so it was hard to get back into the flow. I felt I should have made much more of an impact than I did. It wasn't until the Goodwill Games that I felt I was all the way back. I was in sync. I was exploding again."

Elton returned back to college in the Fall of 1998 as Duke's unquestioned leader in the middle. The two pre-season games had shown the dominant all-around game that Elton possessed.

The National Media began to move Elton into the very upper crust of the country's top players following his stellar performance at the Goodwill Games during the summer.

The awards soon followed, from being named a finalist for the Wooden National Player of the Year Award to his selection as a first-team pre-season All-American. "I expect to just go out and play hard and help propel our team to be the best at the end of the season," Elton said. "There are going to be a lot of people gunning at us and gunning at myself because they see the pre-season accolades, but I'm just going to play and we're going to hopefully play our best. It was a big adjustment playing on another level, but I think I held my own for the first scrimmage. I wasn't dominated or anything, so I think I did all right. It's going to come down to being unselfish, defending and rebounding. With this kind of group, if we're unselfish and we defend and rebound, we'll find a way to win games."

With Elton a member of the Blue Devils, the Duke team fared exceptionally well during the 1998-99 season with an overall record of 33-1. They were undefeated in ACC play at 16 -0, and were a perfect 14-0 in Duke's Cameron Indoor Stadium. When they traveled, the Blue Devils also took the road to perfection with an 11-0 record, with the only blemish coming from playing at neutral sites, where they finished 8-1.

During the first game of the NCAA tournament, better known as "March Madness," Elton exploded onto the court and led his team to a 99-58 rout of Florida A&M. He scored a team-high 17 points and completely dominated post play. Elton could have scored more and posted bigger game numbers, but Duke coach Mike Krzyzewski imposed his own mercy rule on Florida and pulled his starters from the contest.

Whether he would become the first Duke player to leave school early for professional basketball riches --would be decided not by him alone, but by Elton and his mother, who everyone says, was her son's guiding light, his protector, the main reason that he was more respected at Peekskill High for his manners and his A average than for his slam dunks. "She instilled in me good manners and to always be a nice person," Elton says. "That's the way she was, and I picked that up from her."

Elton would graduate from Duke with honors someday, everyone believed, even if he left to join the MBA, and returned in the future to earn his degree, after buying a nice house for his mother and taking care of his family.

Elton, back from a career threatening injury, was anointed the crown prince of basketball with his unanimous selection as a first-team college All-American. After sitting out most of his freshman year with a foot injury, Elton rebounded in 1998 to become one of the most dominant players in the nation. On March 8, one day after he single handedly led Duke to their third straight Atlantic Coast Conference championship, Elton received all 72 first-team votes from the national media panel charged with selecting All-Americans.

All year long, the college basketball world had been singing the praises of the Blue Devil star and as each day passed his legend seemed to grow even larger.

After having a season average of 17.8 points and 9.8 rebounds per game, the Peekskill native, who was currently immersed in the national tournament, was being surrounded with rumors that he was contemplating forfeiting his next two years at Duke in favor of early entry into the NBA. While there were no denials or confirmations, the mild mannered Elton certainly was indeed developing the profile of a professional basketball player.

On May 27, 1999, it was announced that by consensus, Elton Brand was named to the 1999 college All-Americans team. In addition to his All-American honors, the Duke center also was named the ACC tournament's Most Valuable Player. "It's unbelievable. I'm just elated right now. Just to have been considered for first-team All-American was a special honor. I knew I worked hard and the hard work paid off." Growing up it's one of the things he definitely dreamed of. "I'm definitely a team person and the individual accolades come when the teams wins," said Elton. Also named to the All-American team with Elton was Richard Hamilton of Connecticut and Wally Szczerbiak of Miami. The three of them were named as the final three members of the 1999 USA Basketball Men's Senior National Team, which would participate in the 1999 Americas qualification tournament for the 2000 Olympic games.

The 12-member 1999 USA Men's Senior National Team roster consisted of nine NBA players, who were announced on March 10, and the three non-NBA players. The USA Basketball Men's Senior National Team Committee made the player selections.

Peekskill, New York Fans

Whether Elton Brand continued his college career or chose to pursue the professional ranks, he would always rank as one of Peekskill's favorite sons.

Regina Clarkin O'Leary, writing for the <u>Peekskill Herald</u>, wrote extensively about Elton. She reported that Elton said that when people say he was special, it means a lot to him -- especially if it comes from the fans back home, because they know what he had gone through and they've been around a long time watching him. The fans back home form a huge contingent, wrote Ms. O'Leary, - the Decks, Urbanowiczes, Malaspinas, Brophys, Lewes, Sewelks. They follow Duke on the Internet and buy game tickets months in advance.

Some families even traveled from Peekskill to Duke games and make vacations out of it. "Everybody here had something in common," said Joe DeChristopher, "It's a community thing. It's the talk around the area." DeChristopher's daughter, 13-year-old Amy, met Elton a couple of times. He was very cordial and would autograph pictures and basketballs, DeChristopher said. "He's a good role model. The fact that he's doing real well in school makes it so much better," In 1998, the Peekskill Recreation Department secured tickets to some Duke games in the region and people went on a bus to catch the national collegiate star in action. DeChristopher, a University of Kentucky graduate, said the Duke game in December against his alma mater posed a problem for him. "I had to root for Kentucky, but my wife Janene wouldn't talk to me for a few days."

Elton had fans not only from Peekskill, but from all over the county of Westchester. "He's an exciting player to watch," said Wayne Turner, a mailman in Croton, New York, 10 miles away. Wayne says he's interested in Elton because most people don't get to see a kid come out of high school and make it big. "It's a lot of entertainment." Turner, his wife Diane and their two children, Adam, 15 and Allison, 12, went to West Point in 1998 to see Elton in action. They also went to the Meadowlands and Madison Square Garden to follow Elton. The Olsens and Dwyers of Peekskill also went to the Glen Falls games twice when Elton was playing in the state high school finals.

Jim and Bernadette Olsen of Parkway Place in Peekskill

sent away six months in advance for game tickets to a Madison Square Garden showdown between Duke and St. John's so they could see Elton. "We wouldn't be going if it wasn't for Elton," said Olsen, who retired two years ago from the Bank of New York as a carpenter. Not only did the Olsen's get to see one of the most exciting games of the season -- the contest went into overtime with Duke winning by four points, 92-88 -- but Jim Olsen and his son-in-law, Kevin Dwyer, was interviewed on television. Dwyer was Elton's English teacher at Peekskill High. "We were on television, channel 12, during the game," said Dwyer. "We had signs that said 'Elton's Our Hero' and we would stand up with the signs. The cameraman saw the signs and came over to interview us. After the game, we saw and talked to Mrs. Brand," said Olsen. "She recognized us from seeing us at so many games."

Dwyer and his wife Jean have kept in touch with Elton and they took their sons Sean, Craig and Brian on a trip to Hilton Head -- and then went on to Duke in North Carolina. The Olsen's also went on the trip last spring. The Olsen's and Dwyer's went to the Glen Falls games twice when Elton was playing for Peekskill in the state high school finals. And they traveled to the Meadowlands in New Jersey in December to see Duke play Kentucky. At that game, Duke was winning by about 60 points and the mascot was walking around with an umbrella, saying it was raining Duke points.

Dwyer says, "I like basketball and would go to all the high school games because I enjoyed seeing the kids I had in class. I'm also interested in photography, and I would take pictures of the games and send the photos to Elton and his mother."

In addition to all the fervor, it was thrilling to the fans from Peekskill to see Elton playing on Cameron turf. Jean Tryggestad who follows all of Elton's games said, "He was so impressive and so humble, there isn't a cocky bone in his body. He was kind and attentive and sincere. He doesn't brag, doesn't pump himself up."

But eventually, there was an important factor in the career of Elton that began to be widely discussed as the season progressed. Elton had developed so quickly that talk of him leaving college early for the NBA had already begun.

Elton recalled watching Bobby Hurley play and seeing Duke win consecutive national championships. He would love to follow in the footsteps of his basketball predecessors to win another title for the Blue Devils. But the pressures were building up for him to set a precedent that they did not: leaving early for the NBA.

"It would take extreme circumstances," Elton said. "I want to take full advantage of my Duke education. It takes away from the team; if it loses best players it's just not going to be as good unless it can make it up in recruiting. Players' leaving after two to three years make it a lot harder on the team. The players in the NBA are getting paid millions but the team's going to be struggling."

When asked by the media about the possibility of joining the NBA and being the first Duke player to ever leave early and things like that," Elton said. "I don't look that far into the season, and I'm unproven right now. It's not like, okay, you're a first-team All-American last year so now coming back this year. No, it's none of that. That's definitely another jump ahead the media had made."

"I'm nowhere near the same player I was," says Elton. "I'm stronger, more athletic. I've done weights for the first time. I run the court better. I can put the ball on the floor and slash to the basket from the wing. I can jump over people and create shots. I couldn't do any of that last year."

"My mom wants me to graduate. We're not in dire need financially. But we're not as well off as the Hills, either. It was easy for those guys to stay. It might be harder for me."

Elton was already used to all the talk about his possible move to the pros, but he seemed set on waiting until after the season to think about his future. Though it had nothing to do with him personally, Elton had to live with the legacy of no Duke player having ever left early. He pointed out that each individual's situation was different, and no one was more supportive of him than his coach.

"At the end of the year for all of them, if that's what happens, that's what happens," Krzyzewski said. "Elton has got to prove himself to be a great player this year for the whole season. If he thinks too far ahead, he's not going to improve now." Elton said, "Coach was behind us 100 percent. Ever since his home visit he's been supporting us, and we believe in Coach and he believes in us. He'll probably even help players in their decision and whatever they have to do." For Elton, there was no decision right now. He was still focused on proving himself for a full season and helping lead the top-ranked Blue Devils a few games further than they went last year. He knew he was still a long way from joining the likes of Grant Hill, Christian Laettner and Johnny Dawkins in Duke lore. But at the same time, just the chance to join them was an opportunity not many would ever have. "To me he's a beautiful player to watch," Krzyzewski said. "He's potentially a great player. God gave him special things."

In Durham, Duke's home base, basketball players were expected to be great. But Elton was treated like a child prodigy, a dominant player who could lead Duke for two more years. That's why the biggest question in Durham wasn't whether the heavily favored Blue Devils would win the title, but whether Elton would leave school early for the NBA. "Everybody thinks he's going to go," said Keith Kelly, a senior who plays the trumpet in Duke's pep band. "Everyone's hoping that he stays."

Elton had until May 16th to make up his mind about applying for early entry in the June 30 NBA draft. When Duke played at the Continental Airlines Arena in East Rutherford, N.J., Elton said he was tilting toward staying despite the financial temptation.

"I love Duke," Elton said. "I love the whole team experience right now. That (money) would be there. That's the only way you can let down the temptation a little bit, just knowing that it'll be there and just enjoying yourself right now." In Durham, they would keep Elton for as long as they could. "It's unbelievable," said Joe Alleva, Duke's athletic director. "After games, he stands around and signs autographs. People want to take their picture with him. I'm telling you, the kid was just a model for what a student-athlete should be. He's just the perfect kid. He's like a little bear."

Panzanaro, Elton's coach from high school, speaks to Elton often, and said he enjoyed being a college kid, just playing video games with his roommate, point guard Avery. Elton said, "I love everything about college. I like the classes. I like the basketball. The basketball becomes hard. It's work. But I like the rest of the atmosphere. I like the campus. I like being a student."

Many thought Elton would decide to stay at Duke and improve his game. They said things like, "I think he knows he has a lot more to work on as far as the NBA."

Jay Bilas wrote a very good article about Elton in ESPN. Entitled an "Expert Analysis," Mr. Bilas wrote, "Elton Brand was an intriguing pro prospect. At 6-8, he was undersized for a power forward, yet he runs the floor extremely well and can beat his man down-court to score or establish early post position. He has long arms and huge hands, and he plays bigger than he's listed. Elton

Brand has a great touch, and can score with his back to the basket with simple post moves that would be more refined on the next level.

"He was a "below-the-rim" player, but so was Karl Malone, the NBA player to whom Elton Brand was most often compared. Elton Brand was unorthodox and not always smooth, but he had great success even when keyed upon. Elton Brand was agile and can step out and guard on the perimeter. A big question for Elton Brand was his handling of the double-team. At first he would just bull his way through it, but later in his sophomore season he began to make better and quicker decisions. However, Elton Brand did not react well to the double-teams he saw in the NCAA final against the University of Connecticut, and looked unprepared.

"Elton Brand should be in better condition in the NBA and show even better speed and agility. The questions: Can he show a face-up game and hit the mid-range jumper? Can he guard bigger people inside and cover out on the perimeter?"

Decision to leave Duke

"After reviewing my situation with Coach K and the rest of the Duke staff, I have decided to forego my final two years at Duke University to pursue a career in the NBA."

That's all it took, a one-sentence remark from Elton to end all the speculation about his future. On Wednesday, April 14, 1999, speaking at a news conference held at Duke, Elton Brand, a Blue Devil sophomore, officially ended his tenure among the ranks of college basketball players, opting to make himself eligible for the National Basketball Association's June draft.

Elton was the first player to leave Duke before graduating to become a pro, although two teammates, William Avery and Corey Maggett, made the same decision shortly after he did. But only Elton did it with Krzyzewski's blessing. "He was ready," Krzyzewski said. "But Elton felt somewhat guilty. He and his mom wanted to make sure they aren't offending anyone at Duke."

"It has been a lifelong dream of mine (to play in the NBA) and this just takes me one step closer. I'm going to miss my teammates and the friends I have made. Coach and I felt this was the right decision and at the right time,"

Of course there were other considerations. Elton, who was the 1999 ACC Player of the year as well as the recipient of a host of other Player of the Year awards, was expected to be the top pick of the draft. For Elton, that was a crucial element in the decision-making process.

"That was very important (financial security). I want to take care of my mom and my family. Just to be able to live comfortably has always been a dream of mine," said Elton. Mrs. Brand, who was on hand when her son declared himself eligible for the draft said, "It's a joyous day. It's a good choice. It's him achieving his goals."

Elton has always been about achieving goals. Since his days as a high school basketball player, he has achieved the goals of being a good student as well as a good player. But the goal of success in the NBA comes with many questions, one of which was, was he ready?

On that subject, Elton said, "I'm still not ready physically to actually go out there and play with those guys. But a month or two from now I'll be more prepared. I don't think anyone coming out of college was actually ready to play against those guys. I'll be more prepared once I get there, even more."

Elton 's decision to leave the college ranks was not an easy choice, but it was one he felt he had to make. He said the decision to leave school was made easier with the help of Duke Coach

Mike Krzyzewski. "I was very indecisive because who wants to leave a great program like Duke and what it has to offer. But once I made the decision, Coach K was very happy for me and supported me all the way. That made it easier for me," explained Elton.

One of the issues of concern regarding Elton 's choice to go pro was, what would happen to his education? On that topic Coach K said, "We've (Brand and the coach) already talked about continuing his education in finishing up this semester and enrolling in first term summer school. He'll finish his degree in business. He was one of the most intelligent kids I've recruited at Duke. I've thoroughly enjoyed my time with him and I'm just sad that I won't be able to work with him the next couple of years." Elton had won four national player-of-the-year awards and was the only unanimous pick on The Associated Press All-America team.

His 1998-99 achievements included:

1. Early entry candidate for 1999 NBA draft The first player ever from Duke to announce intention of leaving early

2. Scored in double figures in 53 of his 60 college games

3. Posted double-digit rebounds 24 times and had 22 double-doubles

4. Career field goal percentage of .621 was a school record for players with at least 300 field goals made

5. Ranks fifth on Duke's all-time list with 113 blocked shots despite playing just two seasons

6. Was a finalist for the Naismith Award which was given to the top player in college basketballUSA Basketball's Man of the YearScored an incredible 18 double-doubles, which was double-figure rebounds and points in a single game

7. Scored in double figures in 53 of his 60 college games, posted

   double-digit rebounds 24 times and had 22 double-doubles

8. Career field goal percentage of .621 was a school record for

   players with at least 300 field goals made

9. Ranks fifth on Duke's all-time list with 113 blocked shots

   despite playing just two seasons

10. Consensus National Player of the Year as a sophomore

11. Fourth player in 1990s to be voted unanimous AP First Team
    All-American, joining NBA stars Christian Laettner (Duke),

    Glenn Robinson (Purdue) and Tim Duncan (Wake Forest)

12. 1999 ACC Player of the Year and Tournament MVP

13. Also named to All-ACC, All-East Region and All-Final Four
    and Great Alaska Shootout All-Tournament teams

14. Four-time ACC Player of the Week

15. Led Duke with 17.7 ppg, 9.8 rpg (19th in nation) and 86
    blocks, shooting .620 from the field (fourth in nation)

16. Topped ACC in scoring, rebounding and field goal percentage

    and ranked fourth in blocks

17. Averaged 19.3 ppg and 10.3 rpg in ACC Tournament, 17.0
    ppg, 9.2 rpg, 2.0 spg and 2.0 bpg in six NCAA Tournament
    games

18. Scored in double figures in every game except one and posted 19 double-doubles, including 11 in the last 17 games and five in a row

19. Scored a career-high 33 points against Virginia

20. Led or tied for the team lead in scoring 16 times and rebounding 28 times

21. Grabbed at least 10 rebounds in 20 games, with a career-high 21 against Fresno State, the most by a Duke player since Randy Denton had 25 against Northwestern in 1970

22. Played in 21 games with 18 starts and led team in rebounding at 7.3 rpg

23. Was leading team in scoring at 16.0 ppg prior to injury, finished season third at 13.4 ppg

24. Second on team with 27 blocks, getting at least two in 10

    gamesNamed to All-Tournament Team at Maui invitational

25. Scored in double figures 15 times, with season-highs of 23 points against Chaminade and North Carolina-Greensboro

26. Grabbed season-high 14 rebounds vs. Syracuse in NCAA South Regional

27. Scored in double figures in each of his first seven collegiate games.

USA Basketball named Elton the male athlete of the year for 1998 after leading the USA to a gold medal finish at this year's Goodwill Games. He became the second Blue Devil to win the award. Christian Laettner won the award in 1991 after leading Team USA to a bronze medal in the Pan American Games. Other notable winners of the award include Michael Jordan (1983,

1984), David Robinson (1986), Shaquille O'Neal (1994), and Scottie Pippen (1996). By winning this award, Elton became eligible for the U.S. Olympic Committee Sportsman of the Year Award to be presented in December.

Panzanaro wrote, "Who would have dreamed then, that Elton Brand of Peekskill would be a first-team All-American and a candidate for the National Player of the Year award, after only his sophomore year."

Summer 1999

Elton Brand was one of three college players selected in the Spring of 1999 by **USA Basketball** to play on the US National team that would spend seven days in Orlando before heading to Puerto Rico. Wally Szczerbiak and Richard Hamilton were two outstanding first-round draft picks that would also benefit from the experience of playing on the national team.

Elton stared in amazement at the players practicing on the court. Tim Duncan, Tom Gugliotta, Steve Smith, Vin Baker, Gary Payton, Jason Kidd, Kevin Garnett and Tim Hardaway. "We watched these guys all the time on TV," Elton said after the U.S. National Basketball Team worked out for the first time in preparation for the Pre-Olympic Qualifying Tournament of the Americas.

The coach of the team, Larry Brown, said, "I think they're so lucky. Just being around these guys, being around the older players, the guys who have been through it before. It's going to be a tremendous advantage for them in adjusting to pro ball, I can't imagine what it must be like for Elton to be around Tim Duncan and Kevin Garnett, or Richard Hamilton, as a guard, being around Steve Smith, Allan Houston, Gary Payton, Jason Kidd and Tim Hardaway. I'm going to try to get them to really spend a lot of time talking to the guys about what they need to do and what to expect."

Hamilton, the most valuable player in the NCAA Tournament Final Four as he helped Connecticut beat Elton and Duke in the national championship game, said there's no way to measure how much it means to be part of the national team. "A lot of college guys coming out don't get an opportunity like this.

Sometimes you've got to wait 10 years until you can be on the all-star team to get a chance to play with guys like this."

Elton learned so much just by watching. He said about the opportunity to play that summer; "One thing I did was ask the players questions. What does he do here? What does he do there? I was trying to learn everything, trying to take little bits and pieces from everybody. I was not going to be satisfied with my game, thinking I knew everything, because I didn't."

The team went on to beat Canada in an exhibition game at Orlando Arena, before it went to Puerto Rico where it would open the tournament by beating Uruguay on July 15.

Chuck Slater of the NY Times wrote in July 1999, "Elton Brand, the former Duke University sophomore from Peekskill, goes back to his roots just as strongly as he goes to the basket. A week ago last Wednesday; he was the first selection in the National Basketball Association draft. The terrible Bulls record of 13 wins and 37 losses for the 1998-99 season earned them the No. 1 pick in this summer's NBA draft, and they used it to pick Elton Brand, which would guarantee him $10.7 million the first three years and nearly $4 million more if the Bulls pick up the option year.

"A day later," Slater wrote, "...he was in Chicago, being introduced as the player to lead the Jordan-less Bulls back from the depths to which they had sunk last year. Last Monday, he left to practice in Orlando, Fla., with the United States Men's Senior National Team before he took part in an Olympic qualifying tournament in Puerto Rico.

"And in between, Brand, now his hometown's newest millionaire, spent all his free time in Peekskill, New York, at and around the Dunbar Heights garden apartment complex where he still lived with his mother and his brother, Artie. One can still see the metal-netted basket in the nearby playground, which provided an always-big-for-his-age youngster with a goal that would propel him around the world.

"Elton has been out seeing the world and the world's been stopping by to see him" was the way it was put by Mrs. Brand, a single parent who raised two boys who went to college and stayed out of trouble.

"People who know Elton say he's still the same guy, despite the national magazine covers, and the big minutes on ESPN. He still calls his Peekskill buddies when he gets a moment. He wants to hear about them.

"He's just a regular kid --with all the hype and everything," former Peekskill teammate Trevon Telford said. "He knows not to let it go to his head." In the summer of 1998, Elton even found time to work at Panzanaro's weeklong basketball camp, unmoved by his star power.

"He doesn't try to shy himself away from the person he was," said Mark Carter, a student at Peekskill High and a fellow camp counselor. "He accepts the fact that a lot of the little kids look up to him. He's there to show them the right path to go. When he's home, it's like the president was coming to town," Carter said.

In Michael Jordan's last seven full seasons, the Bulls won six championships. Without him, they finished 13-37 last season. Nobody was expecting Elton to totally fill the biggest shoes in basketball history, but many expect that his presence on the Bulls would make a tremendous difference.

"We look forward, not back," said David Falk, who was Jordan's agent and was now Brand's. "Let's not talk of the next Michael Jordan but of the first Elton Brand." Before turning pro, Elton spoke with his good friend from Peekskill, Gov. George E. Pataki, who told him to "do what's best for your family." He got the same advice from the renowned Duke coach Mike Krzyzewski. "He's a sure thing," Krzyzewski said. "In the pros, Elton would change from the center position he manned for Duke to power forward for the Bulls. He would continually go up against athletes taller than himself. No problem."

"People who characterize him as just a power player are so wrong," Krzyzewski said. "He can face the bucket, as a power forward does, and has the ability to put the ball on the floor. He would be unbelievably versatile in the pros."

And unbelievably in shape. The Charlotte Hornets, who picked third and thought they might have a shot at Elton, worked him out. Coach Paul Silas has a drill in which players are fed the ball in a stationary position and dunk it repeatedly. Most players can do about 10 straight dunks, he said Elton did 20 and was not breathing hard.

In preparation for the pros, Elton even hired a personal trainer. It paid off in the multimillion-dollar contract, which the first draft choice picks automatically receive through an agreement between the league and the players' association. Jerry Krause, general manager of the Bulls, said, "He's just an outstanding person."

Elton has made a big leap, but his feet were still on the ground. "In the forefront of my plans was to buy a house for my mom," he said. "She was very special in my life. But for my first year in Chicago, I would like to have her out there with me. I'll need all the support I can get."

During his weigh-in for the Bulls there were some rumors around that he was really 6 foot 51/2, not 6 foot 8. "Teams made a big deal about it," Elton said. "When it was my turn to get measured, it was like, 'O.K., it's Elton, shoes off, socks off, head straight' because there were so many rumors." Elton was so wide-bodied and muscular that he looks shorter. But the tape measure said 6 foot 8. "He's 6-8 'and 275 pounds, and his arm span was wider than some small planes. He's also got the biggest, softest hands I've ever seen," said Bulls general manager Jerry Krause.

The Associated Press reported on July 2, 1999 that when Elton Brand's mother held his new Chicago Bulls jersey for the first time, a huge grin crossed her face and she let out a gleeful laugh as she shook the shirt. Elton said, "I just wanted to come in and see all the trophies," he said, glancing back at the six championship trophies at the Bulls' Practice facility. "I was just in amazement. It's a very special place with all the banners hung up. I was in awe."

But for all the magazine covers he graced and the awards he picked up last year, the national college player of the year said there are still some things people haven't seen.

"I think the general managers and coaches were pleasantly surprised at my perimeter skills and my face-the-basket game," he said. "I didn't get to showcase that much at Duke. But I didn't have to with Avery and Trajan Langdon out there hitting."

People would expect a lot from him, but Elton said they always have. "It's going to be a lot of pressure, but I'm looking forward to the challenge," he said. "At every level, I've had to face pressure and criticism and such, but I always prevailed."

The Bulls were counting on it. After going from dynasty to dust heap, the Bulls were looking for Elton to be the cornerstone of their rebuilding effort. "Just don't start calling him the next Jordan. Or Dennis Rodman. Or anyone else, for that matter," said David Falk, agent for Jordan and Brand. "I think the important thing was not to compare the future with the past."

Elton knows the transition to the NBA might be difficult. He was, after all, just 20 years old, and the NBA was a long way from the Atlantic Coast Conference. Then there's the city of Chicago, which was looking for someone to make the post-Jordan hangover go away.

He was not used to traveling and living away from home, and his mother would come to Chicago with him for at least the first year. He also got a pleasant surprise when the Bulls drafted one of his old AAU buddies, Ron Artist, with the 16th pick.

Artest and Elton played together on the Riverside Church AAU team for three years, including one spectacular season when it went 64-1. They once talked about going to the same college. And now that they were together again, they once sat up late at night talking about how far they've come and how their lives were about to change.

Eleanor Frey, Elton's guidance counselor at Peekskill High and a confidante of the Brands', sometimes worries that NBA hangers-on would zero in on Elton's innocent side. But she's confident his mother would keep him on his path. "Daisy was so focused and knows what he needs," Frey said. "I'm amazed at Elton's ability to handle everything that goes on around him. Yes, he's got his game face on the court, but what a smile when he comes off it. You can see his character in his smile. It's a million-dollar smile, to go with the million-dollar character, to go with the talent that would sooner or later make Elton a multi-millionaire."

Elton said that he learned more lessons at the Tournament of Americas qualifier for the 2000 Olympics the last two weeks in Puerto Rico than he did in the last 10 years. Did the NBA talent impress him? Definitely. But awed? No. "They all showed me ways of improving my game," he said. "Tim Duncan, Kevin Garnett, it's definitely going to be tougher for me next year. It was an honor helping the team get to Sydney, but I think it's going to help my game."

It was a world suddenly much larger for the 6-foot-8, 275-pound superstar. At practice in Orlando, he was banging heads with such all-pro basketball players as Tim Duncan, Allan Houston, Gary Payton and Kevin Garnett. Elton said he learned a few tricks of the power-forward trade from his teammates while in Puerto Rico. "Everything came so fast, but I'm happy with my decision."

When Elton arrived in Chicago for the signing of his contract he didn't go to the Berto Center in a souped-up, bass-booming Hummer. He didn't require an all points bulletin to be located. He didn't wear a silk shirt open to the navel and piercings in every imaginable body crevice. All he did to commemorate the signing of a three-year deal worth $10.7 million was reach down and kiss his mother. This was in the doorway of the Deerfield facility, where Michael Jordan and various other legends have passed through hundreds of times. And if you had been there to see Mrs. Brand break down and cry when they parted, you might have cried, too.

"I love you! I love you!" she said, kissing her son one, two, three, four, maybe 10 times on the cheek. "Call me, call me, call me, call me."

"I'll get you that microwave, Mom, don't worry," replied a grinning Elton, off to catch an airplane that would take him to Utah for the summer league and onto the rest of his promising life.

The microwave would be part of a more elaborate gift package, of course. "A house, a car, whatever she likes," Brand said a few minutes earlier.

A mother's plan had come full circle. "This has always been a dream of mine, standing here as a member of a team like the Bulls," Elton said. "Now the thing was to make sure my mom was happy. She has worked so hard to keep me happy."

His character was so sound, his focus and approach so grounded, Elton single-handedly might calm the outrage about underclassmen turning pro. He's certainly more mature at 20 than Dennis Rodman was at 38. "Elton was a terrific young man," Jerry Krause, the owner of the Bulls, has said every day this summer. "I have yet to hear a single soul, in or out of basketball, argue the point."

The scrutiny would be very intense for Elton; more difficult than anything he ever had to endure as a college or high school star. Elton knows this. "Everybody's going to be gunning for me," he said. "I have to show them I can play. We're in a rebuilding process, but I'm thinking of getting with my teammates and getting into the playoffs. I can't wait to get started. Just seeing the organization, the coaching staff and my teammates, I could see myself being here a long, long time."

He was known in Chicago for his tremendous work ethic, which along with his attitude were considered two of his major assets. All the players had a key to the Berto Center, but unlike most players, Elton was already coming in for solitary workouts that lasted as late as midnight. Guard Randy Brown said that Elton was going to wear that key out. "He's the biggest gym rat I've ever seen." Elton did not mind the extra practice and work. He knew that such effort was the price of success and personal progress.

On July 25, 2000 Elton played in the Magic Johnson charity basketball game in Los Angeles. Just 24 hours after arriving from Puerto Rico, where he played for the United States in the Tournament of Americas Olympic qualifying, Elton Brand made his professional debut July 27th at the Delta Center in Salt Lake City. Elton was there to work out during the Rocky Mountain Revue summer leagues in Salt Lake City, games that didn't count because they were pre-season.

Elton didn't have to be there. The Bulls were ready to excuse him because he had just played for Team USA in the Olympic qualifying tournament in Puerto Rico. But when the games ended, Elton called the Bulls General Manager Jerry Krause and coach Tim Floyd to inform them that he would meet the team in Salt Lake City. Elton felt a little guilty for missing the first game at the mini-camp at the Berto Center in Chicago. Showing his sense of humor, Elton said, "I found out they lost the first game by 21 points without me out there. I knew I wanted to be out there and that they needed me." His teammates had dropped a 75-54 decision to the Minnesota Timberwolves on the tournament's opening day.

Elton said, "It's very important right now to get to know my teammates and get a chance to be able to play with them. The thing to remember was that how you function and try to coexist on the court was important once the season starts. There wasn't a better way to do that than to come in here."

Elton really wasn't expected to play in all the games. The plan was for him to practice with the team and possibly play in just one game.

After one practice and a brief scrimmage, however, Elton was in uniform playing center and contributing 14 points and seven rebounds before fouling out in the Bulls' 73-67 victory over the Utah Jazz. Elton scored 10 points in the final seven minutes when the Bulls wiped out a 50- 45 deficit and rallied past Utah. Even some members of the defeated Utah Jazz were impressed with Elton. Todd Fuller said of Elton, "He's a good player. He started to play more aggressively down the stretch. They were constantly getting him the ball. That seemed like it helped his confidence and aggressiveness." In his second game in the series, Elton scored 11 points and grabbed nine rebounds as the Bulls squeezed past Milwaukee 76-62.

Rusty LaRue, one of the Bull guards who led the team in scoring in the first two games had nothing but good words for his new teammate. "He's doing great. I think anybody who has watched the games sees that he's strong inside and gives us a presence inside. He catches the ball well and was able to finish around the basket."

"It was a great learning experience," said Elton, "I don't know too many of the plays yet, but..." He did pretty good for not yet knowing the plays.

Tim Floyd, the Bulls coach who was watching Elton's debut from the stands was overjoyed. "My first impression was that our fans in Chicago were going to love his enthusiasm. He's a high-energy player and, if the fire keeps burning, maybe he's a guy we can plug in there for a long, long time."

Elton fit right in with the Bulls as if he was one of their seasoned players. He cheered on his new teammates, slapped and was slapped himself on the backside. He made faces with them when they made mistakes, and inspired the entire team with his overall intensity and energy.

The Bulls assistant coach Jim Wooldridge could not praise Elton enough. After watching Elton play in Utah, he said, "You can see he's contagious and it's a positive contagious. It's not just because of his play. He's got such a high gear to him. He's enthusiastic, he loves to play, and I mean that with all sincerity. There's no fake there. Not everybody has that kind of personality. He does, and that's been a big lift to these kids going through this training camp." (He was speaking here of high school stars who were invited to the camp.)

It was the decision of Bull vice president Jerry Krause to draft Elton instead of Maryland guard Steve Francis, UCLA point guard Baron Davis, Rhode Island's Lamar Odom or Miami's Wally Szczerbiak. Floyd believes, "There's going to be a big scope on him, no doubt about that. That's one of the reasons Jerry picked him. He thought Elton could handle it. We feel like he's going to be rock-solid for us."

Elton's response to all this praise was his usual display of humility and inner confidence, "It's going to be tough. There would be pressure and a lot of high expectations. But I'm looking forward to being a cornerstone to the rebuilding process."

Against the Bucks on July 29th, Elton defended the 6-8, 280-pound Robert "Tractor" Taylor, which was not an easy task. Elton's response was, "It's just getting me ready. This was what I'm going to see. It's definitely a benefit. I'm glad I came, just to get that competition. It's good to play against these veterans and get a good run." It was now clear that Elton had already made a very positive impression on the minds of his veteran teammates. It was now evident that Elton Brand's presence on the Bulls was making a big difference.

Veteran guard B.J. Armstrong, was impressed with the composure of his new teammate. "Elton was like a 40-year-old man trapped inside a 20-year-old. He comes in and just does his work. He's on time and does all the things that you would think a player a little older would do. He's very mature." Another teammate, center Would Perdue said, "He's like a sponge. He's eager to learn as much as he can about the game."

Bulls forward Dicky Simpkins said, "But he already seems to know a lot. He's so mature in his attitude toward the game."

The Bulls unveiled their No. 1 draft pick On October 14, 1999 at the United Center in a preseason game against the

Denver Nuggets. Elton sounded more like a veteran who understands the monotony of the preseason rather than a bright-eyed 20-year-old who just completed his sophomore year at Duke.

All Elton had to say about the upcoming game was," Maybe I'll be nervous, but maybe not. I am excited to finally get out there and play against someone other than my teammates."

Elton had been a force during the first week of training camp. He had demonstrated a soft touch on short jumpers and a powerful determination around the basket.

It would be interesting to watch him compete against Denver's 6-9, 220-pound Antonio McDyess, who was considered one of the top forwards in the league. "It's the first game of the preseason," said Elton, so I'm not sure he'll play a lot, and I'm not sure I'll play a lot. But if I do get a chance, I'll try to defend him and play against him because he was one of the better forwards in the league. He's going to be a challenge for whoever guards him. If it's me, I'm looking forward to the challenge."

The last time Brand played at the United Center, he led Duke to a convincing victory against DePaul on Feb. 24, 1999. "It's just a great, big arena," he said. "It can get loud at times, but I'm used to playing in big arenas, and I'm looking forward to it."

For Elton Brand, it was an important opportunity to publicly showcase his highly acclaimed skills, and Elton did not disappoint his followers. In his very first game in the preseason, Elton was the driving force for the Bulls, providing a clue to his NBA future by collecting 18 points, 11 rebounds, five assists and two steals.

"Whoever was hot, we were just going to try to get him the ball," said Elton, who was 8 for 14 from the field. "I really felt like his shot selection was great," said coach Tim Floyd of Elton. "His body was unique and he does a great job of creating separation with his body. He has a nice little fade away, and he also has got the power moves."

The Bulls trailed 47-43 at the half before outscoring Denver 20-14 in the third quarter to gain control. They went on to claim an exciting 86-84 victory over Denver.

"I just try to be a positive person about everything. I know there were a lot of pressures on being the number one draft pick, and I'll accept them as a challenge. They'll just make me work harder to help my team as effectively as I can. I hope to blossom more on the pro level than I did on the college level." If he does as well as he hopes he would he would probably be picked Rookie of the Year, which was one of his personal goals. But whatever the Bulls lack, that's what Elton wants to supply. When he was asked to predict a headline for the 1999-2000 season, his response was, "Brand saves game by recovering loose ball."

"Off the court I have to grow up very fast. My mother isn't there any longer, or coaches or even my Duke support team. I'm on my own, by myself. It's not like being on campus anymore."

Some experts did not expect the Bulls, to even make the playoffs. They were supposed to be in a rebuilding process after a disastrous 1998-99 season. Elton's response to this was, "I think we'll use it as a motivating factor that not much was expected from us. We rookies and new guys, we just don't know any better. We're naive. If we play hard, you're going to see some wins."

"When you've worked all your life for this and dreamed all your life for such a special moment, when it comes, it just feels very special," Elton said. "I'm very eager to get in here and get started. I'm looking forward to the great experience that's going to come." There was a very good possibility that Elton could be selected as the 12th man on the Dream Team for the Olympics in the summer of 2000.

"It was a super challenge to follow Michael Jordan," said Elton. "It's a lot of pressure playing for the Bulls with the heritage and the championships. I'm ready to take that challenge, to go hard and fight and prove all the naysayers wrong. I think I would be remembered as the person who brought the Bulls back."

Brand Starts Charitable Foundation with
The Giving Back Fund

On July 6, 2001, Elton announced that he would create a charitable foundation with The Giving Back Fund. Elton's appreciation for the communities where he has lived and played basketball was what has inspired him to want to give back.

The Elton Brand Foundation would support nonprofit organizations, which have a commitment to at least one of the following three areas:

- After-school educational programs (computer classes, literacy, math and science, etc.)

- Fostering and encouraging children's participation in sports

- Support of single parents

Grants would be distributed in Chicago, IL, where he was playing for the Bulls; Peekskill, NY, his hometown; and Durham, NC, where he played for Duke University.

Brand announced his first grant to Chicago Commons (Mile Square Center); a nonprofit social service agency located just two blocks from the United Center. To further support its mission of developing life management skills for kids and young adults, a grant of $10,000 would be made to support Chicago Commons' computer technology center and intramural sports program. Chicago Commons creates programs that build self-sufficiency, strengthening individuals at key stages of their lives from child development to job-preparedness.

In establishing his foundation, Brand said, "As a professional athlete, I am in a position to have an impact on issues that were important to me. I have been lucky in my young career, and I'm very excited to have this opportunity to establish a foundation so I can start giving back to my communities."

Marc Pollick, founder and president of The Giving Back Fund commented, "What Elton was doing was nothing less than extraordinary. For a player so early in his career to wear the mantle of role model and philanthropist so readily was a remarkable thing. I applaud him and I salute his efforts."

The Elton Brand Foundation is a member of The Giving Back Fund's community of foundations. The Giving Back Fund is a national nonprofit organization based in Boston dedicated to helping professional athletes, entertainers, and individual donors create and manage charitable foundations for philanthropic giving. The Fund provides professional expertise in every aspect of foundation management and charitable planning. The scope of services offered by The Giving Back Fund and its partners include strategic and legal consultation, financial planning and investment management, administrative support, grant making, public relations, web site development and maintenance, and assistance with special events. The Fund also provides a full array of services to already existing foundations. Charity organizations seeking more information may contact The Giving Back Fund at (617) 557-9910 or via mail at 54 Canal Street, Boston, MA 02114.

Elton Brand Launches MathNSports Club for Youth In Partnership with MathMastery

On July 12, 2001 Elton made the following announcement - "The key to being successful in math was finding the beauty and utility within the subject. And that often means relating math to real-world interests, like sports. Combining sports statistics and basic math skills can add to students enjoyment and learning, help build confidence, and strengthen math skills."

In a press conference, Brand commented on his partnership between MathMastery and The Giving Back Fund to form the MathNSports Club. The MathNSports Club presents basic math skills such as addition, subtraction, multiplication and division, as well as more advanced skills such as fractions, decimals, algebra and word problems, within the context of sports. "It's an exciting and realistic way to reach students and teach math," Brand noted. The announcement as made as part of Elton Brand Youth Day in Peekskill, featuring free basketball clinics for youth ages seven to 14 and a free concert for families with Lil' Romeo.

To access the MathNSports Club, go to www.mathmastery.com and click on the Elton Brand caricature. Students who join MathMastery's MathNSports Club receive a free certificate of enrollment featuring a picture of Elton. As students progress through the courses, Elton would be appear on their "Progress Reports" with accolades for a job well done. As an added incentive, students who complete the various math courses would receive a series of posters featuring Elton.

The MathNSports Club was the second of MathMastery's interest-specific math clubs for youth. The MathNMusic Club, featuring Justin Timberlake of NSYNC and Britney Spears, was launched in June. A portion of the proceeds generated from the MathNSports Club subscriptions would benefit the Elton Brand Foundation and a portion of the proceeds from the MathNMusic Club subscriptions would benefit the Britney Spears Foundation and the Justin Timberlake Foundation. All are members of The Giving Back Fund's family of foundations.

MathMastery provides rigorous math content, support materials and fun family activities to increase student achievement in math. MathMastery was founded on the award winning *Core Concepts in Science and Mathematicsä* math programs, recognized by the U.S. Department of Education as an "exemplary" educational program. For more information about MathMastery, or to preview the new MathNMusic Club, visit MathMastery on the Internet.

The Giving Back Fund is a national, nonprofit organization that encourages and facilitates charitable giving by professional athletes, individuals in the entertainment industry and others. The Fund provides professional expertise in every aspect of foundation management and charitable planning. For more information, visit The Giving Back Fund at www.givingback.org.

To see a slide show of 100 pictures of Elton on the LA Clippers, type the following website address into a search engine: http://clippers.topbuzz.com/modules/gallery/slideshow.php?set_al bumName=elton_brand

Elton with the Clippers

The Bulls, and Beyond

- Named to the USA Basketball 2002 Men's World Championship Team.

- Made his first career All-Star appearance (first Clipper since Danny Manning - 1994), replacing an injured Shaquille O'Neal on the 2002 Western Conference All-Star Team.

- Ranked first in the NBA in total offensive rebounds (396) and offensive rebounds per game in 2001-02.

- Named to the 1999-2000 Schick All-Rookie First Team.

- Named the co-winner of the 1999-2000 Schick Rookie of the Year Award, along with Steve Francis.

- Named the MVP of the 2000 Schick Rookie Challenge, notching 16 points and 21 rebounds.

- Named the Schick Rookie of the Month for January and February 2000.

- Recorded his first career double double, scoring 21 points and grabbing 12 boards against the Atlanta Hawks on 11/6/99.

- As a sophomore at Duke, Brand garnered almost every award imaginable. After leading Duke in scoring (17.7 ppg), rebounding (9.8 rpg) and blocked shots (86), Brand was the consensus National Player of the Year and a unanimous First Team All-American selection by AP, as well as the 1999 ACC Player of the Year and USA Basketball's Man of the Year.

- Despite only playing two seasons at Duke, Brand left his mark on the Blue Devil record books. His career field goal percentage mark of .621 was the highest ever for players with at least 300 made, and he ranks fifth with 113 career-blocked shots.

Career Highlights

- Averaged 21.0 points and 15.0 rebounds a game for the 2003-2004 season with the Clippers. .583% FG.

- Averaged 18.5 points and 11.3 rebounds a game during 2002-2003, with a .502% FG.

- 2002 Men's World Championship Team.

- Made his first career All-Star appearance (first Clipper since Danny Manning - 1994), replacing an injured Shaquille O'Neal on the 2002 Western Conference All-Star Team.

- Ranked first in the NBA in total offensive rebounds (396) and offensive rebounds per game (5.0) in 2001-02.

- Named to the 1999-2000 Schick All-Rookie First Team.

- Named the co-winner of the 1999-2000 Schick Rookie of the Year Award, along with Steve Francis.

- Named the MVP of the 2000 Schick Rookie Challenge, notching 16 points and 21 rebounds.

- Named the Schick Rookie of the Month for January and February 2000.

- Recorded his first career double double, scoring 21 points and grabbing 12 boards against the Atlanta Hawks on 11/6/99.

- As a sophomore at Duke, Brand garnered almost every award imaginable. After leading Duke in scoring (17.7 ppg), rebounding (9.8 rpg) and blocked shots (86), Brand was the consensus National Player of the Year and a unanimous First Team All-American selection by AP, as well as the 1999 ACC Player of the Year and USA Basketball's Man of the Year. Field goal percentage mark of .621 was the highest ever for players with at least 300 made, and he ranks fifth with 113 career-blocked shots.

- Elton was the NBA's top offensive rebounder the past two seasons with an average of 5.0 in 2001-02 and 4.6 in 2002-2003.

Elton Brand is an inspiration to all of us who at times would rather stay in bed than get up and exercise, or go to school or work, or read that book, or simply meditate. Always remember that each of us has been blessed with some type of genius. Elton found and developed his on the basketball court. He worked very hard from a young age to become the best in what he wanted to do. He is recognized now as one of the best basketball players in the world, and all of his friends and fans are proud of him.

It's very difficult and takes a lot of work to become a professional athlete or even a professional entertainer, but the important lesson that Elton shows us is that the earlier our talents are identified and developed, the greater our chances will be of becoming successful in that field. Be it a plumber, a lawyer, a secretary, a schoolteacher, a nurse, an astronaut, a barber, a cook, an actor, or a writer.

The important thing is that you are happy in your chosen occupation. The sky is the limit for each of us as it is for Elton Brand. Go for it!

AUTHOR'S BIOGRAPHICAL NOTE

Offie C. Wortham grew up in the same town as Elton Brand and graduated from Peekskill High School a generation before. Besides being a writer he has been a social scientist, college professor and administrator, advisor to the FBI, scientist in advanced research at IBM, community organizer and change agent, civil rights leader, inventor, senior missile and space technician, editor, researcher, and life coach. He is happily married to his loving wife Vivian, and has three wonderful daughters and five healthy and beautiful grandchildren.

Fern Penna Biographical Note

Fern Penna was an early bloomer who knew at age 15 that it took work and a strong will to succeed in life. While still a teen, he started his own construction business when everybody told him he would fail. A born leader, he started a church and a youth group in the Catskill Mountains at age 12. Later in life, he became an architect and a very successful business and political consultant. Fern Penna is now running for president of the United States because he always wanted to better mankind and bring our children to a safe heaven where they would have a foundation to stand on for the future. Fern Penna currently sits on many different boards worldwide; Moller International, H.E.A.R.T., Help America's Education, Inc, among others. He is also currently a member of a board dedicated to the environment with Pete Seeger. See his website on: www.penna04leadership.com.

Full book description (The Elton Brand Story)

Elton Brand is a living role model and a shining example of the success of the American Dream. From very humble beginnings in a public housing project in Peekskill, NY, Elton emerged as the most sought after basketball player in the United States, if not the world. He became a star at Duke, and went on to become the first player ever to leave that college to join the NBA. He was successful with the Chicago Bulls and went on to the Los Angeles Clippers, where in September of 2003 he was offered a contract of $82,000,000.

This exciting and easy-to-read book takes you from his home town, where as captain he led the local high school team twice to the state championships, to his selection as All-American and eventually, National Player of the year in the NBA. This book is the first of many that will be written about this great basketball player, and outstanding individual.

BRIEF DESCRIPTION

Elton Brand is a living role model and a shining example of the success of the American Dream. This is the story of how he went from a public housing project to an NBA contract of $82,000,000.